Disney **PRINCESS**

CELEBRATE
with Jasmine

Plan an *Aladdin* Party

Niki Ahrens

Lerner Publications ◆ Minneapolis

Lerner Publications Company
An imprint of Lerner Publishing Group, Inc.
241 First Avenue North
Minneapolis, MN 55401 USA

For reading levels and more information, look up this title at www.lernerbooks.com.

Main body text set in Billy Infant.
Typeface provided by Sparky Type.

Library of Congress Cataloging-in-Publication Data

Names: Ahrens, Niki, 1979- author.
Title: Celebrate with Jasmine : plan an Aladdin party / Niki Ahrens.
Description: Minneapolis : Lerner Publications, [2020] | Series: Disney Princess celebrations | Audience: Ages: 6-10. | Audience: Grades: K-3. | Includes bibliographical references and index.
Identifiers: LCCN 2019010970 (print) | LCCN 2019017969 (ebook) | ISBN 9781541582774 (eb pdf) | ISBN 9781541572751 (lb : alk. paper)
Subjects: LCSH: Party decorations—Juvenile literature. | Children's parties—Juvenile literature. | Handicraft—Juvenile literature. | Jasmine (Fictitious character from Disney)—Juvenile literature. | Aladdin (Motion picture)—Juvenile literature.
Classification: LCC TT900.P3 (ebook) | LCC TT900.P3 A44 2020 (print) | DDC 745.594/1—dc23

LC record available at https://lccn.loc.gov/2019010970

Manufactured in the United States of America
1-46542-47587-6/18/2019

Table of Contents

A Magical Party

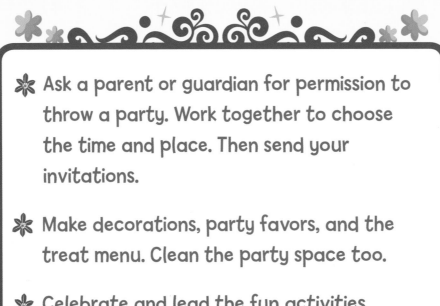

Jasmine dreamed of exploring new things. Her journey to see more was magical. Plan the *Aladdin* party of your dreams! Here's what you'll need to do:

* ❋ Ask a parent or guardian for permission to throw a party. Work together to choose the time and place. Then send your invitations.

* ❋ Make decorations, party favors, and the treat menu. Clean the party space too.

* ❋ Celebrate and lead the fun activities you've planned!

* ❋ Afterward, clean up and send thank-you notes to your guests.

Party Host Tips!

* Ask guests about food allergies before the party. Be respectful when planning.

* Prepare by getting your party supplies ready before celebrating.

* Be safe when prepping food! Wash your hands, and ask an adult for help with kitchen tools.

* Kindly include every guest in the fun.

* Show gratitude by thanking everyone for coming.

* Be earth-friendly! Recycle all materials that you can after the party.

Flying Invitations

Just as Jasmine frees her caged birds, you can send bird invitations flying to your party guests.

Materials

- white paper plates

- scissors

- bright paper muffin liners

- white glue

- orange construction paper

- googly eyes

- pen

1. Fold a paper plate in half. Cut along the fold line. This will make two bird bodies.

2. Flatten a muffin liner, and then fold it in half. Cut along the fold line. This will make two wings.

3. Glue a wing to the center of a bird body.

4. Cut a small triangle bird beak from the orange paper. Glue the beak and a googly eye to your bird.

5. On the back of the bird, write your important invitation details in pen. Include the party date, time, and location.

6. Make one invitation for each of your guests. Then send your birds flying!

Party Tip! Be Earth-Friendly

Be kind to the planet, and use scrap paper to decorate! Cut leftover orange paper into tiny pieces. Sprinkle the colorful confetti on your party table.

Rajah Print Decorations

Make bright handprint art inspired by Jasmine's best friend, Rajah. These decorations will liven up your party space!

Materials

- medium paintbrush

- orange tempera paint

- white construction paper

- black marker

- scissors

- masking tape

1. Use the medium paintbrush to paint the palm side of your hand with the orange paint.

2. Spread apart your fingers, and carefully stamp your hand on the white construction paper.

3. Turn the paper so the stamped fingers are pointing toward you. These are the tiger's legs. The thumbprint should be pointing to the side as a tail. On the opposite side from the tiger tail, paint a circle for a head and add triangle ears.

4. If you want to make more than one print, repeat steps 1 to 3 to create as many Rajah decorations as you'd like.

5. Wash your hand, and let the orange hand stamps dry completely.

6. Add a face and stripes to your tigers using the black marker.

7. Cut out the tigers, and tape them around your party space.

Apple Doughnut Treats

Pretend that you are at the Agrabah marketplace, and share apple donut treats with your guests.

Materials

- cutting board

- slicing knife

- small spoon

- 1 butter knife for each frosting or spread

- small bowls and spoons for each topping

Ingredients

This recipe serves 6 to 8.

- 3 apples

- lemon juice

- frosting

- nut or sunflower butter spreads

- toppings such as sprinkles, raisins, mini chocolate chips, and little candies

1. Wash your hands and rinse the apples. Place each apple on its side on the cutting board.

1.

2. Have an adult slice each apple into 5 to 6 round discs.

2.

3. Press the small spoon around the core portion of each apple disc to cut out a hole. This will make your apple look like a donut. Sprinkle your apples with a little bit of lemon juice to keep them fresh for when your guests arrive. Put the toppings in small bowls.

3.

4. Set out apple rings, frosting, nut butter, knives for spreading, bowls of toppings, and spoons! Be sure to avoid your guests' allergies with your spreads and toppings.

5. Invite your guests to wash their hands before starting. Then they can create apple donuts with their favorite spreads and toppings.

Party Tip! Did You Know?
Apple trees come from central Asia and the Middle East. That's why the market in Agrabah had apples!

Magic Carpet Placemats

Weave colorful Magic Carpet placemats with your guests.

Materials

- 3 sheets of 9 x 12 inch (23 x 30 cm) construction paper in 3 colors per person

- rulers

- pencils

- scissors

- glue sticks

- yarn and markers (optional)

1. Fold a sheet of construction paper in half, matching its shorter sides. Using the ruler, draw a line in pencil across the open end of the paper 1 inch (2.5 cm) from the edge.

2. Keeping your paper folded, cut strips about 1 inch (2.5 cm) thick from the folded edge to the line you drew on the open end. Unfold your weaving mat, and set it aside.

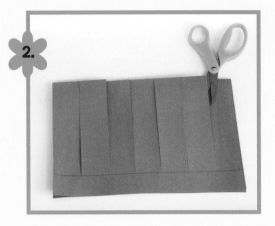

3. Take out two more sheets of differently colored paper. Cut them into strips about 1 inch (2.5 cm) wide, working across the shorter sides of the paper.

4. Tuck a paper strip under the mat's first strip, and then pull it over the second strip. Repeat this motion until you get to the end of the strip. Push that strip to one side of your mat.

5. Take a new color strip and begin by going over and then under. Push that strip next to the first one. Keep weaving strips in this pattern until your mat is full.

6. Glue the strip ends to the weaving mat.

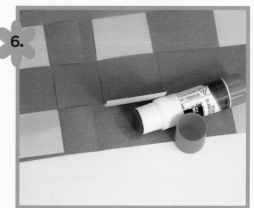

7. If you want, you can decorate your placemat with yarn and markers.

Party Tip! Did You Know?

Middle Eastern carpets are made of woven knots. The carpets often have repeating patterns. Some have symbols such as leaves and animals. The world's oldest handwoven carpet is about three thousand years old.

Toss Ahead Game

Aladdin and Jasmine need to stay *one jump ahead*. Play this toss game to see if you can stay ahead of the "palace guard."

Materials

- 3 clean hand towels

- 6 to 9 rubber bands

- scissors

- cardboard

- markers

- masking tape

- 3 plastic mixing bowls

- yardstick

1. Set up the game before your guests arrive. Take the towels and roll them into balls. Wrap at least two rubber bands around each towel ball to be sure it keeps its shape.

2. Cut cardboard into 3 squares about 4 inches (10 cm) across. Use the markers to write large numbers 1, 2, and 3 on the pieces of cardboard.

3. Tape one sign to the inside of the back rim of each plastic bowl. The numbers should be easy to read.

4. Place a 12-inch (30 cm) piece of tape on the floor of the game area.

5. Place the 1-point bowl 3 feet (0.9 m) in front of the tape. Place the 2-point bowl a little farther than the first one. Place the 3-point bowl a little farther than the second. The bowls should line up with the 1-point bowl closest to the tape.

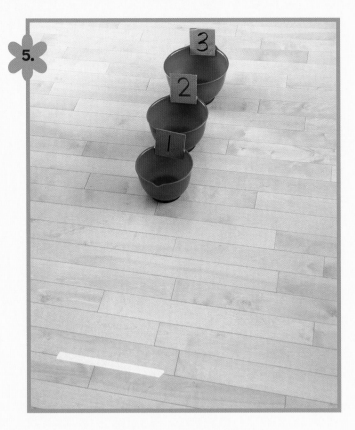

6. At the party, ask your guests to line up behind the tape, facing the bowls. The player in front will play the role of the palace guard. The palace guard gets 3 tosses. Keep track of the number of points he or she earns.

7. Everybody else takes a turn doing 3 tosses. Players that earned more points than the palace guard got away. Switch the player who is the palace guard, and play again. Remember to cheer on every player!

7.

Party Tip! Be respectful

It's okay if a guest chooses not to try the game. When you give guests the choice to play or not, that can help them feel more comfortable at your party.

Abu Pencil Topper Party Favors

Abu is Aladdin's best friend and becomes a loyal friend to Jasmine too. Send Abu pencil buddies home with your guests.

Materials for One Favor

- 1 brown pipe cleaner

- 1 unsharpened pencil

- craft glue

- 1 medium-size brown pom-pom

- 2 small brown pom-poms

- 2 googly eyes

- scissors

- yarn

- 1 small purple pom-pom or craft gem

1. Tightly wrap a pipe cleaner around a pencil from its eraser toward the unsharpened point. Once you've wrapped about half of the pipe cleaner, stretch the remaining half out as Abu's tail. You can curl the tip of the tail if you want.

2. Push the coiled pipe cleaner up so the top is just above the eraser.

3. Add craft glue to the top of the coil, and attach a medium-size brown pom-pom. Hold it in place until the pom-pom sticks. Then gently slide the coil so the pom-pom is at the eraser end.

4. Glue 2 small brown pom-pom ears to each side of the medium pom-pom. Glue 2 googly eyes and a small yarn smile on the front of Abu's head.

5. Add a purple pom-pom or gemstone for Abu's fez hat. Make a party favor for each guest.

Genie Thank-You Notes

Genie grants wishes to help Aladdin be part of Jasmine's world. Send Genie magic to your guests for being a part of your party!

Materials

- 1 sheet of 9 x 12 inch (23 x 30 cm) blue construction paper for each guest

- drinking glass

- pencil

- crayons

- white glue

- googly eyes

1. Fold a sheet of blue paper in half to make a card.

2. Place the drinking glass upside down in the center of the card's cover. Trace around the rim of the drinking glass with the pencil to make a circle.

3. Using the black crayon, draw 2 ears, hair, and a beard for your Genie. Outline the rest of your circle with the crayon.

4. Glue the googly eyes to Genie's face. Draw a nose and a smile. You can give Genie eyebrows and a golden hair band too!

5. Make a Genie card for each guest. Inside each card, write a thank-you message, and then sign your name.

You helped make the party magical. Thank you for coming!

Let Your Plans Take Off

Jasmine's sense of adventure led her to new heights and sights. Where will your party-planning curiosity lead you?

You can have fun dreaming up new ideas with your imagination. You'll have a magical time when you plan the *Aladdin* party that best fits you. Tap into your strengths as Jasmine did, and let your plans soar!

Glossary

comfortable: feeling safe and at ease

confetti: small sprinkles of paper used for decorating

fez: a flat-topped hat that usually has a tassel and no brim

guest: someone who attends a person's event or party

handwoven: woven by people's hands rather than by a machine

host: a person who holds an event or party for guests

loyal: supportive of something or someone in easy and hard times

Middle East: the countries of southwestern Asia and northern Africa

weave: to form a mat or cloth by wrapping materials over and under other materials

To Learn More

BOOKS

Ahrens, Niki. Aladdin *Idea Lab.* Minneapolis: Lerner Publications, 2020. Explore fun STEAM projects inspired by the magic of *Aladdin.*

Felix, Rebecca. *Mini Decorating.* Minneapolis: Lerner Publications, 2017. Decorate small spaces in a big way with tiny details.

WEBSITES

Disney Movies *Aladdin*
https://movies.disney.com/aladdin
Find lots of fun *Aladdin* activities and more.

20 Ways You Loved *Aladdin*
https://ohmy.disney.com/movies/2015/09/25/20-ways-you
-loved-aladdin/
Enjoy some of *Aladdin*'s most memorable moments and characters.

Index

PHOTO CREDITS

Additional photos: Kostikova Natalia/Shutterstock.com, p. 2; Julia Sudnitskaya/Shutterstock.com, p. 3; Olyina/Shutterstock.com, p. 5T; UfaBizPhoto/Shutterstock.com, p. 5B; Victoria 1/Shutterstock.com, p. 7T; Julia Pleskachevskaia/Shutterstock.com, p. 7B. Design elements: Susii/Shutterstock.com; YamabikaY/Shutterstock.com; art_of_sun/Shutterstock.com; surachet khamsuk/Shutterstock.com.